Anonymus

Biennial Report of the Board of Trustees

Alabama Institute for the Deaf and the Blind

Anonymus

Biennial Report of the Board of Trustees
Alabama Institute for the Deaf and the Blind

ISBN/EAN: 9783741177781

Manufactured in Europe, USA, Canada, Australia, Japa

Cover: Foto ©Thomas Meinert / pixelio.de

Manufactured and distributed by brebook publishing software
(www.brebook.com)

Anonymus

Biennial Report of the Board of Trustees

BIENNIAL REPORT

OF THE

BOARD OF TRUSTEES

OF THE

ALABAMA INSTITUTE FOR THE DEAF,

IN CHARGE OF THE

ALABAMA INSTITUTE FOR THE DEAF,

ALABAMA ACADEMY FOR THE BLIND

AND THE

ALABAMA SCHOOL FOR NEGRO DEAF MUTES AND BLIND,

TO THE GOVERNOR.

1892.

MONTGOMERY, ALA.:

SMITH, ALLRED & CO., STATE PRINTERS AND BINDERS.

1892.

BOARD OF TRUSTEES.

OFFICERS AND TEACHERS.

ALABAMA INSTITUTE FOR THE DEAF.

PRINCIPAL:
J. H. Johnson, M. D.

ASSISTANT PRINCIPAL:
J. H. Johnson, Jr., A. M.

TEACHERS.

SIGN DEPARTMENT:
S. J. Johnson, A. B.   Osce Roberts,   Miss A. L. Johnson,
W. S. Johnson,   Miss M. E. Toney.

ORAL DEPARTMENT:
Miss Mary McGuire,   Miss Lois Atwood.

INDUSTRIAL DEPARTMENT:
Osce Roberts.............................. Foreman Printing Office.
M. J. Hingle..Master Mechanic.
W. G. Davirson...Machinist.
John Lennard.....................................Gardener.
Miss Emma Ruppert...................................Seamstress.

DOMESTIC DEPARTMENT:
J. H. Johnson, Jr.,......................................Superintendent.
Mrs. J. H. Johnson, Jr.,......................................Matron.
Miss M. E. Toney.......................................Girls' Supervisor.
Miss A. A. McMillan................................. Housekeeper.
W. G. Davirson...Engineer.

OFFICERS AND TEACHERS.

ALABAMA ACADEMY FOR THE BLIND.

INTELLECTUAL DEPARTMENT :

J. H. Johnson...Principal.
J. H. Johnson, Jr.,..................................Asst. Principal.
W. A. Wilson......................................Senior Teacher.

Miss L. S. Borden,   Miss Rosa Borden.

MUSICAL DEPARTMENT :

J. S. Laverty...Director.
A. W. Williams..Teacher.

INDUSTRIAL DEPARTMENT.

Chas. Petty...Master Shops.
Miss South..Seamstress.

DOMESTIC DEPARTMENT :

W. A. Wilson...................................Superintendent.
Mrs. W. A. Wilson.....................................Matron.
Mrs. B. C. Mills...................................Housekeeper.
J. D. Wilson.....................................Boys' Supervisor.

OFFICERS AND TEACHERS.

ALABAMA SCHOOL FOR NEGRO DEAF MUTES AND BLIND.

INTELLECTUAL DEPARTMENT:

J. H. Johnson..Principal.

J. H. Johnson, Jr.,...................................Asst. Principal.

J. S. Graves...........................Senior Teacher of the Blind.

Robert Spivey..................................Teacher of Blind.

Alfred F. Wood..............................Teacher of the Deaf.

MUSICAL DEPARTMENT:

Robert Spivey...Teacher.

INDUSTRIAL DEPARTMENT:

Robert Spivey..Master Shops.

DOMESTIC DEPARTMENT:

J. S. Graves.......................................Superintendent.

Mrs. J. S. Graves.......................................Matron.

A. F. Wood...Supervisor.

PRESIDENT'S REPORT.

To His Excellency,

THOS. G. JONES,

Governor of Alabama :

SIR :—I have the honor to present herewith the reports of the principal and officers of the State schools for the Deaf and Blind for the years 1891–1892.

In response to the enlightened progress of the age, joined with a spirit of justice, an act of the last General Assembly, appropriated $12,000.00 for the purpose of establishing a school for the negro Deaf-mute and Blind of Alabama.

This school was intended to constitute a department of the Deaf and Blind Institutions of the State, and the act provided that it should be under the control and management of the Trustees of the Institute for the Deaf. Accordingly, with this appropriation of $12,000.00 a handsome and durable brick structure was built with as little delay as practicable.

The building is three stories and basement, with slate roof, well planned for the service intended; and with the attractive site, inviting grounds and enclosure is regarded as a highly valuable addition to the State property.

On the completion of this building the principal promptly organized a corps of teachers with other necessary assistants for operating the school, who began teaching negro pupils January 4th, 1892.

With a part of the fund bequeathed to the Deaf and Blind schools, by the late John Wilson, a handsome printing outfit and a work-shop well equipped with wood-working machinery has been added to the mechanical department of the " Alabama Institute for the Deaf."

Besides imparting valuable service to the pupils by teaching them valuable lessons in mechancical handicraft, this department proves at once a source of convenience and economy to the Institution; since through it all needful printing is done, mattresses and furniture made and repaired besides repairs on the various buildings thereby saving in the aggregate considerable sums of money to the State.

It becomes our painful duty to report the death of our fellow trustee, J. P. Wood, a valued co-laborer, who was ever ready to give his valuable experience and counsel in the interest of the Institution. A tribute to his memory will be found on pages 25–30 of this report.

The report of the Principal shows the disposition of the funds appropriated by the last Legislature together with the money received from all other sources.

An account of the changes in the administration of his office, the promotion of J. H. Johnson, Jr., to the place of Vice-Principal and the employment of additional teachers necessitated by the enlarged field of duties, is also found in his report.

The Institution in all its departments is in a gratifying state of prosperity—bearing on its rolls a larger number of pupils than ever before in its history.

The buildings are all in good repair, while the grounds, gardens and lawns bear ample evidence of the taste, skill and energy presiding in their immediate management.

Briefly, in all its parts and operations the Institution gives continued evidence of the will and ability of the Principal and co-laborers to maintain its acknowledged claim to the front rank of the highest class of deaf-mute and blind education.

Very respectfully your obedient servant,

W. Taylor,

President of the Board of Trustees.

Talladega, Ala., November 10th, 1892.

REPORT OF SECRETARY OF THE BOARD OF TRUSTEES.

TALLADEGA, ALA., Nov. 10th, 1892.

DR. WM. TAYLOR,

President Board of Trustees of the

Alabama Institute for the Deaf.

SIR:—I have the honor herewith to submit the Report of the Treasurer of the Board as required by law for the two fiscal years just passed, ending September 30th, 1892. And also by order of the Board of Trustees the Report of the Principal, as to the management and progress of the three schools under his supervision, for the same period of time.

Respectfully submitted,

J. H. JOHNSON,

Secretary of the Board of Trustees.

PRINCIPAL'S REPORT.

To the Honorable Board of Trustees
of the Alabama Institute for the Deaf.

GENTLEMEN :—The following brief statement of the progress and condition of the several schools, entrusted by you
to my management, covering the two years ending September 30th, 1892, is most respectfully submitted:

THE ALABAMA INSTITUTE FOR THE DEAF.

The Alabama Institute for the Deaf has steadily advanced
along the lines believed by the Principal and your honorable
board best calculated to promote the interests of the deaf
children of the State entrusted to our care.

The health of the pupils has been excellent, no deaths
have occurred and no serions illness of any kind. The sanitary conditions are as good as we know how to make them.

The number of pupils enrolled since date of last report
is—No. of boys, 58. No. of girls, 65. Total 123.

The number present November 10th, 1892, boys, 46, girls,
51, total 97.

We have in the school seven teachers, five manual or sign
teachers and two oral teachers. Of the sign teachers (3)
three are deaf-mutes and (2) two are speaking persons.

School-room appliances are of the best, and good work is
expected and required of our teachers.

This school is now under the supervision of J. H. Johnson,
Jr., Vice-Principal, who assumed the duties of his office at
the opening of the current school year.

This Institution is maintained at a cost to the State of
$217.50 per pupil per annum.

A statement of the quarterly expenditures, for maintenance for the past two years ending September 30th, 1892,
may be seen in another part of this Report. Also a statement in full of all moneys received for maintenance, salaries,
buildings, insurance and repairs, and paid out by the Treasurer of the Board.

CONDITION OF BUILDINGS.

The main building was thoroughly overhauled during the
past summer, the roof, gutters and valleys made almost en-
tirely new ; all exposed metal and wood-work well painted.
Office, parlors, sitting rooms and study rooms re-arranged,
refurnished and painted. The dormitories replastered and
refitted. the school building was also roofed and guttered
anew.

The Wilson Shop building was regutted and the boiler-
room connected with the coal-yard by a brick tunnel 8x8
feet 100 feet long.

The barn, stables and other out-houses were repaired and
painted. The grounds are in good condition, the walks and
drives regravelled and rolled.

THE WILSON SHOP.

The mechanical department for the Institute for the Deaf
is by order of the Board of Trustees called the "Wilson Shop"
in honor of the late Mr. John Wilson of Pike Road, Montgomery county, Alabama, who bequeathed the money which
was used in equipping it. This shop is supplied with planer,
universal wood-worker, band saw, rip and cut-off saws, mor-
tiser, turning lathe, drill press, emory wheels, &c.—also
blacksmith's forge and tools—and cabinet work benches and
tools for twenty boys—the machinery is run by a forty-horse
power, high speed, Automatic Buckeye Engine.

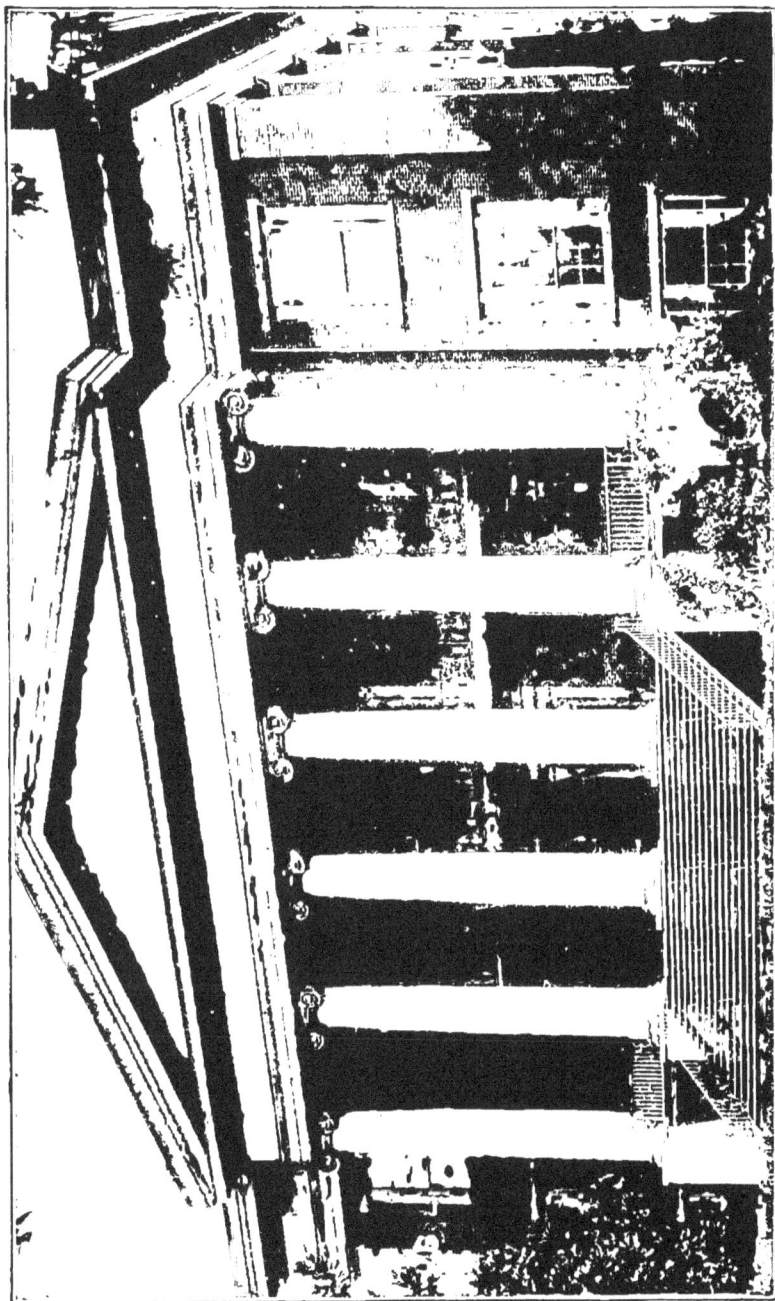

ALABAMA INSTITUTE FOR THE DEAF, AT TALLADEGA.

THE PRINTING OFFICE.

The printing office just opened at date of last report, has been most successfully run, and the "*Messenger*," our Institution newspaper—which compares favorably with other papers of its class—has been regularly issued weekly during the school terms for the last two years.

CONFERENCE OF PRINCIPALS.

This Institution was represented at the Conference of Principals, Trustees and Superintendents of Institutions for the Deaf in America, which was held at the Colorado Institution for D. D. and B. at Colorado Springs in August last, by the Principal and one of the Trustees, Mr. J. B. McMillan.

The conference, the largest and one of the most interesting ever held, was entertained by the Colorado Institution, in the most liberal and hospitable manner.

Many subjects of greatest interest to the cause of Deaf-mute Education in America received the careful consideration of the Conference.

STEAM HEATING AND SANITARY SEWER.

Only one of the buildings on the premises of the Institute for the Deaf is heated by steam, *i. e.*, the Wilson shop and printing office. The boiler house is in the basement of this building and is large enough to hold the boilers necessary to heat the other three buildings. The stack contains a seperate flue for that purpose.

The Board, by resolution passed at the annual meeting in June last, requests our representatives in the next General Assembly to ask the State for a sum sufficient to buy and put in the boilers and steam piping, coils, &c., necessary to heat all the buildings by steam, and for an additional sum to connect our premises with the sanitary sewerage system of the city which has a sewer already laid along the street fronting the Institute.

The sum of three thousand dollars will be sufficient for these purposes.

The saving annually in coal and the safety from fire are reasons why we should have the steam heat.

Although the system of sewers and cesspool which we now have, seems to work well, it is only a matter of time, when the health of the pupils will be endangered thereby. We are not able out of the small annual allowance for repairs and insurance to pay for improvements of this kind. Our maintenance fund $217.50 per pupil per annum, is required, every dollar of it, to carry on the work of the Institute creditably.

THE ALABAMA ACADEMY FOR THE BLIND.

In this school the number of pupils enrolled since date of last report is—No. of boys 48. No. of girls 41. Total 89. The number present November 10th, 1892, boys—, girls—, total 56.

Applications have been made for the admission of others and the number will probably reach 65 by the beginning of next quarter.

At the beginning of the current school year, Mr. W. A. Wilson was placed in charge of the Academy as Superintendent and senior teacher—and Mrs. Grace E. Wilson appointed matron.

Since the date of last report Miss Rosa Borden has been added to the list of teachers in the literary department, and Mr. John Wilson has been appointed Boy's Supervisor.

The Academy is well equipped in all of its departments and is doing good work.

The buildings although'quite new have, during the past summer, received careful attention and some greatly needed additions made. Two rooms have been added and a two story porch erected on the east front. Not being in reach of the sanitary sewer of the city, a cess-pool was built and water closets put in and connected therewith. A cesspool though not a very desirable thing to have under any circumstances, is the best we can do, and seems to work well.

During the fall of 1891 there were several cases of fever at the Academy all of which however recovered, only one case being protracted.

The mechanical department of this school, under the management of Mr. Petty, has been steadily carried on, and some good workmen, mattress makers, cane seaters, collar and mat makers, turned out.

The musical director, Mr. J. S. Laverty and his assistant, Mr. A. W. Williams, have been successful in keeping up the high standard of this branch of the school, and infusing new interest in the study of music.

ASSOCIATION OF AMERICAN INSTRUCTORS OF THE BLIND.

This school was represented at the session of the Convention of American Instructors of the Blind which was held at Brantford, Ontario, in July last by Messrs. J. H. Johnson, Jr. and W. A. Wilson. These gentlemen report that the occasion was a most agreeable and profitable one.

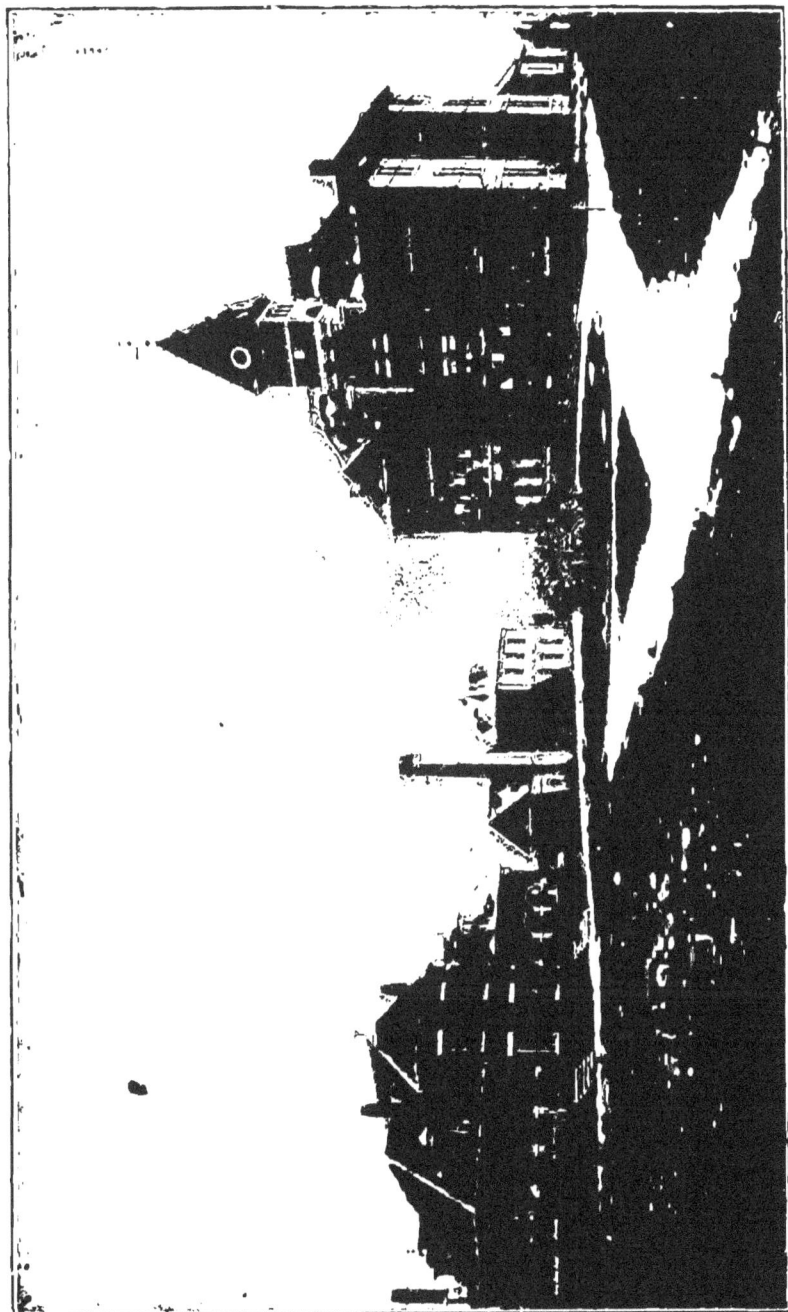

ALABAMA ACADEMY FOR THE BLIND, AT TALLADEGA.

ALABAMA SCHOOL FOR NEGRO DEAF-MUTES AND BLIND.

Since the date of last report "The Alabama School for Negro Deaf-Mutes and Blind" has been established by legislative enactment, and placed under your supervision and my general management.

For this purpose the sum of $12,000.00 was appropriated for erecting buildings—the building site having been donated —and the sum of $6,000.00 appropriated annually for maintenance, until the number of pupils shall exceed thirty, "after which time the school shall be maintained on the per capita plan as for the Academy for the Blind."

The buildings for this school have been erected on a lot embracing six acres, situated due south of the Alabama Academy for the Blind and one-half mile distant from it.

The main building is three stories high with basement, well built with good hard brick, trimmed with stone and covered with slate. The necessary outbuildings, servants house, barn, baths, water closets, &c., are built of wood and painted, the whole furnished in a plain but good and substantial manner.

The amount appropriated by the act, establishing this school, has been sufficient for the purpose and has been expended as shown by the report of the treasurer accompanying this report.

This school was opened for the reception of pupils January 4th, 1892.

Mr. J. S. Graves was placed in charge as superintendent and senior teacher of the blind with Mr. Robert Spivey, a graduate of the Academy for the Blind, as assistant.

Mr. Alfred F. Wood, late principal of the day school for deaf-mutes in Toleao, O., was placed in charge of the school for the colored deaf.

Mrs. J. S. Graves, the wife of the Supt., was appointed matron.

The Institution is thoroughly furnished for its work, and those in charge well qualified for the places they fill, and the work has progressed thus far in a very satisfactory manner.

There are present to day November 10th, 1892, Deaf-mutes 13. Blind 21. Total 34.

In order to interest as far as possible the colored people in this school, the Board of Trustees authorized the appointment of a board of visitors composed of six of the most prominent colored citizens of Talladega, of which Rev. J. P. Barton is chairman. This board is requested to visit the school whenever they may see proper to do so and examine into its management and condition.

Respectfully,

J. H. JOHNSON,

Principal.

IN MEMORIAM.

IN MEMORY OF J. P. WOOD.

At the regular quarterly meeting of the Board of Trustees of the Alabama Institute for the Deaf, held April, the 4th, 1892, the following resolutions were unanimously adopted :

Resolved, That the Board of Trustees are deeply moved, and filled with regret by the recent death of JAMES P. WOOD, a member of this Board, and extend to the family of the deceased Trustee, and to the people sincere condolence in their bereavement.

Resolved, That the double service of JAMES P. WOOD, as Trustee and Treasurer of the Board, has been marked by fidelity to the convictions of his duty to the interest of the Institution, and by promptness and accuracy in the wise control of its funds.

Resolved, That the Secretary of the Board transmit to the family of the deceased, a copy of these resolutions, together with the tribute prepared by the special committee, appointed for that purpose by the Board, and cause the same to be published in THE MESSENGER and the city papers.

Attest: J. H. JOHNSON,

Sec'y Board of Trustees.

TRIBUTE OF RESPECT.

The inevitable hand of death has again invaded our Board and taken from us a faithful, just and venerated co-laborer. Our associate and fellow-Trustee, JAMES P. WOOD, died at his home, the 3d of March 1892, in the midst of his family and friends, honored and regretted by the people in every community, in which his sterling merits were known. It now becomes our sad, but grateful duty, to commemorate, and place upon the records of the Institution, something of his history, his noble traits and virtues. JAMES PINCNEY WOOD was born in St. Clair County, Alabama, March 10th, 1823— having at the time of his death, nearly reached the Psalmist's allotted years of the life of man. His parents were of that sterling, honest, thrifty and sturdy class of people, who came to Alabama, in her territorial days, reclaimed her wilderness wastes, and changed them into productive farms and plantations. At the time of his birth, they owned and cultivated the plantation on which less than ten years before stood Fort Strother, noted in the history of our country, as General Jackson's base of operations in his triumphant campaign against the Creek Indians, in which the power of that savage, but the brave and war-like tribe was forever broken. This was the home of the Woods for more than a generation, and it was on this historic ground that JAMES PINCNEY spent his childhood and youth, drawing from the inspirations of his surroundings, those high attributes for which his life was conspicuous. The Coosa River flows through the plantation in its rapid course through the lower part of the "Ten Islands," and on it the government lock, known as No. 3, now stands. His education was not classic, but limited to the English studies. For a brief time, in his early manhood, he taught school with marked success, in the neighborhood of his old home.

On the 7th of August, 1846, he married Miss Maria N. Rogan, a lady of refined culture who survives him, with four beloved and most estimable daughters. In 1847 he moved to Tippah county, Mississippi, where he engaged in farming. Remaining in Mississippi perhaps two years he returned to his native state, and after another year or two, devoted to agriculture, he finally settled in Alexandria, Calhoun county, and there began a prosperous and successful career as a merchant. After the close of the war, in 1865, he removed to Talladega, where he engaged in mercantile pursuits, on a more extended scale, first under the name and style of Wood & Bro., and more recently under the firm name of J. P. Wood & Company.

As a merchant he was eminently successful, of unquestioned integrity and probity; always just and accurate and liberal in his dealings, he won the confidence of the trade and commanded extensive and lucrative patronage. He was a man of rare business judgment and sagacity, made judicious investments, and while not wealthy in the modern sense of the term, he amassed a very large competency. He was rich in the wisdom born of his own observations, reflections and experience, and was almost infallible in judgment. A high moral sense was the ruling power in his whole life; it pervaded his entire nature, and was strong and acute. Indeed, in every relation to his fellowmen he was guided by an inflexible fidelity to his moral convictions. For many years he was a member of this Board—having been appointed to the place by Governor Cobb in 1884 to succeed Hon. M. H. Cruikshank, deceased, and since the death of Colonel A. G. Storey, our honored Treasurer. All of his fellow-trustees can attest the value of his ripe judgment, the fidelity and cordial support, which he always accorded to the interest of the Institution. Broad and liberal in his views, he was conservative and economical in practice, highly essential qualities in those having control of public institutions.

In personal appearance, Mr. Wood was of fine physique. In statue he was above six feet and well developed in manly form. In repose, his expression was grave, but bright and radiant when animated. His voice was soft and pleasant for a man of his masculine mould. His carriage was erect, measured and dignified. In social qualities he was affable and gracious, perhaps somewhat taciturn, but never austere in manner, under a grave exterior was concealed a vein of subtle humor and sparkling repartee. Gifted with great equanimity of temper, he was usually cheerful and seldom depressed in spirit. In personal habits, he was remarkably abstemious, never addicted even to the use of tobacco in any form, and while not a votary of total abstinence he was never known to abuse the use of wine or other strong drink, and never indulged excessively in the pleasures of the table. For the greater part of his irreproachable life, he was a member of the Presbyterian Church, and possessed all the virtuous fortitude of the christian, joined with the calm philosophy of the stoic.

But he is now departed from the walks of life no more to be seen of men. He has passed from death unto life, into the realms of eternity, there to dwell for all time to come in that blissful abode of just men made perfect. His tall, erect and familiar form reposes in the cemetery of the city where he spent so many years of his useful life, his memory honored and enshrined in the hearts of a grateful community. In all respects he came up to the full measure of the poet's ideal "an honest man is the noblest work of God."

W. TAYLOR,
G. A. JOINER,
J. B. McMILLAN,
Committee.

APPENDIX.

J. B. McMILLAN, Treasurer,

In account with

THE ALABAMA INSTITUTION FOR THE DEAF,

THE ALABAMA ACADEMY FOR THE BLIND,

THE NEGRO SCHOOL FOR THE D., D. AND B.

		INSURANCE AND REPAIR FUND.		
1890				
Oct.	9	To cash from State Treasurer.	$ 1,000 00	
1891				
Oct.	7	" " " "	1,000 00	$ 2,000 00
		CREDITS.		
1890				
Nov.	21	By cash J. H. Johnson, Jr	500 00	
Dec.	20	" J. H. Johnson, Prin...............	500 00	
1892				
May	9	" Z. H. Claedy & Son.........	154 89	
June	6	" J. H. Johnson, Jr., Supt	461 00	
Sept.	30	By balance	384 11	$ 2,000 00
		To balance	$ 384 11	

J. B. McMILLAN, Treasurer,

In account with

THE ALABAMA INSTITUTION FOR THE DEAF;

THE ALABAMA ACADEMY FOR THE BLIND,

THE NEGRO SCHOOL FOR THE D. D. AND BLIND.

1891		BUILDING FUND.		
May	15	To cash from State Treasurer............	$ 6,000 00	
Oct.	7	" " " "	6,000 00	$ 12,000 00
		CREDITS.		
May	15	By cash paid express charges...........	4 50	
	21	" " J. H. Johnson...., ...	25 00	
		" " T. S. Plowman...........	450 00	
June	24	" " Geo. Kramer.............	390 90	
July	9	" " Geo. Wheeler.............	212 00	
	21	" " Building Committee	4,000 00	
Sept.	15	" " " "	917 60	
Oct.	14	" " " "	4,000 00	
Dec.	8	" " " "	2,000 00	$ 12 000 00

2

TREASURER'S ACCOUNT.

J. B. McMILLAN, Treasurer,

In account with The Alabama Institution for the Deaf,

The Alabama Academy for the Blind, and the

Negro School for the Deaf, Dumb and Blind.

1890			
Sept. 30	To balance on hand...................... $	1,671	27
Oct. 9	cash from State Treasurer	7,225	00
1891			
Jan. 7	State Treasurer.....................	7,448	75
April 8	State Treasurer	7,448	75
June 16	Shop.	29	85
July 4	Clothing	3	50
9	State Treasurer.................	7,448	75
Aug. 12	Clothing. &c	361	22
Oct. 7	State Treasurer	7,621	25
10	Clothing, &c....................	139	80
Nov. 16	" Shelby county	66	75
Dec. 18	Shops...........................	25	00
1892			
Jan. 7	Clothing.......................	6	00
	State Treasurer	9,680	62
Feb. 11	J H. Johnson, Jr., exchange horse...	30	00
12	Shops, ...	60	00
16	Clothing.......................	30	00
April 6	State Treasurer....................	9,565	62
May 6	Shops...........................	50	00
June 11	J. H. Johnson, railroad fare........	1	02
28	Clothing, &c...................	189	05
17	Shops.........................	30	00
July 2	State Treasurer	9,565	62
18	Mrs. A. E. Johnson, clothing.......	40	00
19	Rent, cottage....................	20	00
	Total............................... $	68,757	82

CR.

1890			
Oct. 6	By cash paid Mrs. M. J. Williams	75	00
9	J. H. Johnson, Jr.. Supt.	875	00
	" "	1,184	24
10	" "	225	00
	Mrs. E. G. Johnson	75	00
	J. S. Graves.....................	225	00
	Miss L. S. Borden...............	150	00
	J. S. Laverty...................	187	50
	A. Williams....................	75	00
	Amount carried forward .... $	3,371	74

TREASURER'S ACCOUNT—Continued.

1890	Amount brought forward.................$	3,371 74
Oct. 10	By cash paid Express charges..............	6 15
	J. H. Johnson, Principal	2,000 00
	" "	536 19
	" "	375 00
	Mrs. E. A. Johnson.............	125 00
	Miss A. L. Johnson	150 00
	B. C. Brown.................	150 00
	Sallie Mabry	75 00
	S. J. Johnson.................	150 00
	W. G. Daverson.................	125 00
15	Miss M. E. Toney.................	100 00
27	W. S. Johnson	125 00
1891		
Jan. 7	J. H. Johnson, Jr., Supt.	1,238 90
	" "	800 00
	" "	225 00
	Mrs. J. H. Johnson...............	75 00
	L. S. Borden	150 00
	J S. Laverty	187 50
	Express charges...................	5 60
	J H. Johnson, Principal	2,000 00
	" "	1,229 18
	" "	375 00
	W. S. Johnson	125 00
	W. G. Daverson.	125 00
	Miss Amelia McMillan............	75 00
	Kate Fish	150 00
	B. C. Brown.................	150 00
	Osce Roberts......	125 00
10	J. S. Graves..................	225 00
	A. Williams.....................	100 00
	Miss Sallie Mabry	100 00
	Mrs. E. O. Johnson..............	125 00
	S. J. Johnson..................	187 50
	Miss A L Johnson..............	150 00
	M. Field.....................	75 00
	M. E. Toney..	100 00
16	J. H. Johnson, Principal............	233 58
	J. P. Wood..	37 50
Mar. 18	J. H. Johnson, Principal..........	600 00
April 8	Express charges	3 75
10	Miss Kate Fish	150 00
	B. C. Brown......	150 00
	A. A. McMillan	75 00
	Osce Roberts	125 00
	J. H. Johnson. .. ..•.....	375 00
	J. H. Johnson, Principal	2,000 00
	" "	367 48
	S. J. Johnson....	187 50
	Miss M. Field..................	100 00
	Sallie Mabry.................	100 00
	W. G. Daverson.................	125 00
	Amount carried forward.................$	20,017 57

TREASURER'S ACCOUNT—Continued.

1891	Amount brought forward.	$ 20,017	57
April 10	By cash paid J. P. Wood	37	50
	W. S. Johnson	125	00
	Miss M. Toney	100	00
	A. L. Johnson	150	00
	Mrs. E. A. Johnson	125	00
	J. S. Laverty	187	50
	A. Williams	100	00
	J. S. Graves.	225	00
	J. H. Johnson, Jr., Supt.	1,292	01
	" "	700	00
	" "	225	00
	Mrs. E. J. Johnson	75	00
	Miss Lydia Borden.	150	00
July 9	Express charges	3	75
	Miss B. C. Brown.	150	00
	"	150	00
	Sallie Mabry	100	00
	"	100	00
	Kate Fish	150	00
	"	150	00
	A. L. Johnson	150	00
	A. A. McMillan	100	00
	Mrs. E. A. Johnson	175	00
	S. J. Johnson	187	50
	J. H. Johnson.	375	00
	" Principal	202	25
	" "	2,000	00
	W. G. Daverson	125	00
	J. P. Wood	37	50
	W. S. Johnson	125	00
	Osce. Roberts	125	00
	Miss M. E. Toney	100	00
	L. S. Borden	150	00
	A. Williams	100	00
	J. H. Johnson. Jr.	225	00
	Mrs. E. G. Johnson	75	00
	J. S. Graves	225	00
	J. S. Laverty	187	50
	J. H. Johnson. Jr., Supt.	1,003	18
	" "	1,000	00
Oct. 8	Express charges.	10	95
	J. H. Johnson.	375	00
	" Principal	2,000	00
	" "	816	16
	Mrs. E. A. Johnson	125	00
	Miss A. L. Johnson	150	00
	S. J Johnson	187	50
	W. S. Johnson	125	00
	Miss A. A. McMillan	100	00
	M. E. Toney	100	00
	W. G. Daverson	125	00
	J. P. Wood	37	50
	Amount carried forward	$ 35,133	37

TREASURER'S ACCOUNT—Continued.

1891			
	Amount brought forward	$	35,133 37
Oct. 8	By cash paid Osce. Roberts,.	125 00	
	J. H. Johnson, Jr., Supt.	1,100 00	
	" "	1,054 68	
	" "	225 00	
	Mrs J. H. Johnson	75 00	
	J. S Graves.	225 00	
	Miss L. S. Borden.	150 00	
	J. S. Laverty	187 50	
	A. Williams.	100 00	
Dec. 14	J. H. Johnson, Jr., Supt.	300 00	
18	J. H. Johnson, Principal	500 00	
1892			
Jan. 8	Express charges.	9 55	
	J. H Johnson, Principal	276 17	
	" "	2,000 00	
	" "	375 00	
	Mrs. E. A. Johnson	125 00	
	Miss A. L. Johnson	150 00	
	S. J. Johnson	225 00	
	W. S Johnson	175 00	
	Miss Lois Atwood	150 00	
	A. A. McMillan	100 00	
	M. E. Toney	125 00	
	Osce. Roberts	180 00	
	J. P. Wood.	37 50	
	W. G Daverson	125 00	
	J. H. Johnson, Jr	793 43	
	"	1,500 00	
	"	250 00	
	Mrs. J. H Johnson.	125 00	
	Miss L. S. Borden	150 00	
	A. Williams.	125 00	
	J. S. Graves	225 00	
	J. S. Laverty	200 00	
	J. H. Johnson, Principal	90 00	
	J. S. Graves, Supt.	1,000 00	
March 1	W. H. Dillon, Ins.	20 00	
April 7	Express charges.	4 80	
	J. H. Johnson, Principal	2.000 00	
	" "	895 60	
	J. P. Wood	37 50	
	J. H. Johnson.	375 00	
	S. J. Johnson	225 00	
	W. S Johnson.	175 00	
	Mrs. E A Johnson	125 00	
	Miss A. L Johnson	150 00	
	M. E. Toney	125 00	
	M. McGuire..	175 00	
	A A. McMillan	100 00	
	Lois Atwood	150 00	
	Osce. Roberts,.	175 00	
	W. G Daverson	125 00	
	Amount carried forward.	$	52,545 10

TREASURER'S ACCOUNT—Continued.

1891		Amount brought forward	$ 52,545	10
April	7	By cash paid J. H. Johnson, Jr , Supt.	1,500	00
		" "	851	58
		" "	250	00
		Mrs. J H. Johnson	125	00
	8	J. S. Laverty	200	00
		W. A. Wilson.	250	00
		Miss L. S. Borden	150	00
		J. S. Graves, Supt	1,000	00
		" "	139	18
		Mr. and Mrs. J. S. Graves	250	00
	9	A. F. Wood.	150	00
		Miss Rosa Borden	75	00
		A. Williams	125	00
June	8	Miss Lois Atwood	150	00
		M. McGuire	175	00
		A. F. Wood.	150	00
July	2	Express charges	12	95
	4	J. H. Johnson. Principal	2,000	00
		" "	281	90
		Miss L. S. Borden	150	00
		Rosa Borden.	75	00
	5	W. S. Johnson	175	00
		S. J. Johnson	225	00
		Miss A. L Johnson	150	00
		Mrs. E. A. Johnson	125	00
		W. G. Daverson	125	00
		Osce. Roberts.	180	00
		J. H. Johnson, Jr., Supt.	1,500	00
		" "	130	57
		" "	250	00
		Mrs. J. H. Johnson.	125	00
		W. A. Wilson.	250	00
		A. Williams	125	00
	6	J. H. Johnson.	375	00
		Miss A. A. McMillan	100	00
	8	J. S. Laverty	200	00
	9	J. S. Graves, Supt.	700	00
		Mr. and Mrs. J. S. Graves	250	00
	27	Miss M. E. Toney	125	00
Sept.	9	J. H. Johnson, Principal.	1,000	00
		J. H. Johnson, Jr., Supt.	500	00
			$ 67,216	28
		Balance brought down	1,541	54
		To amount forward.	$ 68,757	82
Sept.	30	To balance on hand	$ 1,541	54

STATEMENT OF QUARTERLY EXPENDITURES FOR MAINTENANCE

ALABAMA INSTITUTE FOR THE DEAF.

Quarter ending	Dec. 31, 1890	$3,229 18		
"	" Mar. 31, 1891	2,367 48		
"	" June 30, 1891	2,202 25		
"	" Sept. 30, 1891	2.816 16—	$10,615 07	
Quarter ending	Dec. 31, 1891	2,767 17		
"	" Mar. 31, 1892	2,895 60		
"	" June 30, 1892	2,281 80		
"	" Sept. 30, 1892	3,687 20—	11,631 77	

$ 22,247 84

ALABAMA ACADEMY FOR THE BLIND.

Quarter ending	Dec. 31, 1890	$2,613 90		
"	" Mar. 31, 1891	2,092 01		
"	" June 30, 1891	1,778 18		
"	" Sept. 30, 1891	2,054 68—	$ 8,538 77	
Quarter ending	Dec. 31, 1891	2,193 43		
"	" Mar. 31, 1892	2,351 58		
"	" June 30, 1892	1,630 57		
"	" Sept. 30, 1892	2,863 46—	9,039 04	

$ 17,577 81

ALABAMA SCHOOL FOR NEGRO DEAF-MUTES AND BLIND.

Quarter ending	Mar. 31, 1892	$1,139 18	
"	" June 30, 1892	728 90	
"	" Sept. 30, 1892	1,035 94—	$ 2,904 02

ALABAMA INSTITUTE FOR THE DEAF.

LIST OF PUPILS ENROLLED SINCE DATE OF LAST REPORT

No.	Name.	County.
1	Adams, Charles	Lowndes.
2	Alston, Nat	Marengo.
3	Amberson, Earnest	Etowah.
4	Autry, Emma	Colbert.
5	Baldwin, Raymond	DeKalb.
6	Bailey, Ada	Madison.
7	Batson, Mary	Jefferson.
8	Bell, Pauline	Dallas.
9	Benagh, Hill	Limestone.
10	Benagh, Julia	Limestone.
11	Bennett, Mary	Calhoun.
12	Blanchard, Georgia	Talladega.
13	Blansit, Alice	DeKalb.
14	Blansit, Della	DeKalb.
15	Black, Linnie	DeKalb.
16	Box, Mattie	Henry.
17	Brocato, Joe	Jefferson.
18	Brannon, Willie	Talladega.
19	Brust, Lottie	Madison.
20	Cagle, Henry	Marion.
21	Caldwell, Chalmar	Talladega.
22	Caldwell, Loachie	Talladega.
23	Carré, May	Sumter.
24	Carré, Robert	Sumter.
25	Castleberry, William	Talladega.
26	Chandler, Oscar	Etowah.
27	Connell, Francis	Jefferson.
28	Crabb, Robert	Madison.
29	Crapps, Andrew	Monroe.
30	Crapps, Sallie	Monroe.
31	Daly, Harry	Jefferson.
32	Delay, Agnes	Jefferson.
33	Dickinson, Nellie	Pike.
34	Dobing, Alice	Walker.
35	Dorlan, Phelan	Mobile.
36	Dorlan, Viola	Mobile.
37	Durant, Martin	Mobile.
38	Elrod, Willie	Jefferson.
39	Fleming, Jeff	Clarke.
40	Folmar, Pearl	Pike.
41	Fountain, Joe	Perry.
42	Gould, Lyman	Mobile.
43	Hall, Burrell	Shelby.
44	Hawkins, Ada	Lamar.
45	Haynie, Eva	DeKalb.
46	Hamilton, Fanny	Calhoun.
47	Harwood, Earnest	Perry.
48	Harwood, Percy	Perry.
49	Heaslett, Laura	Talladega.
50	Heaton, Asa	Jefferson.
51	Horn, Martin	Talladega.

41

LIST OF PUPILS, DEAF—Continued.

No.	NAME.	COUNTY.
52	Hughes, Mamie	Talladega.
53	Jarrell, Ada	Chambers.
54	Johnson, Ida	Coffee.
55	Johnson, Mattie	Chambers.
56	Johnson, Willie	Pike.
57	Keeble, Lizzie	Jackson.
58	King, Bessie	Walker.
59	King, Lou	Walker.
60	King, Sallie	Walker.
61	Knighten, Edward	Choctaw.
62	Kenigsthal, Arthur	Dallas.
63	Ledbetter, Isaac	Talladega.
64	Lemons, Jesse	Talladega.
65	Levy, Earnest	Jefferson.
66	Logan, Beulah	Bibb.
67	Logan, Dee	Bibb.
68	Logan, Mary	Bibb.
69	Lovelace, Emma	Lauderdale.
70	McClellan, Dan	Talladega.
71	McGill, Ida	Talladega.
72	McLendon, Luther	Jefferson.
73	McKendree, Lizzie	Lee.
74	Middlebrook, Bennie	Montgomery.
75	Morris, Estin	Tallapoosa.
76	Mullen, Mary	Marion.
77	Parks, Sallie	Pike.
78	Pearson, William	Tallapoosa.
79	Peters, William	Jackson.
80	Peters, Henry	Jackson.
81	Pollard, Eddie	Marshall.
82	Powe, Mary	Talladega.
83	Powell, Susie	Jefferson.
84	Pritchett, Martha	Calhoun.
85	Quarles, Dolph	Russell.
86	Quarles, Willie	Russell.
87	Ray, Minnie	Clay.
88	Ray, Winnie	Clay.
89	Rives, Virginia	Monroe.
90	Roberson, Foster	Limestone.
91	Rountree, Marion	Pike.
92	Roach, Etoile	Lauderdale.
93	Ruppert, Winnie	Jefferson.
94	Sanders, Gertrude	Elmore.
95	Seaborn, Jennie	Jackson.
96	Smith, John	Clay.
97	Smith, Peter	Lee.
98	Sowell, William	Limestone.
99	Stephens, Edgar	Dallas.
100	Sullivan, Eulela	Washington.
101	Sullivan, Idumea	Washington.
102	Sullivan, Lyman	Washington.
103	Sullivan, John	Jefferson.
104	Sullivan, Pink	Jefferson.

42

LIST OF PUPILS, DEAF—Continued.

No.	Name.	County.
105	Taut, Fmily	Talladega.
106	Tidwell, Lena	Walker.
107	Thornton, George	Randolph.
108	Thornton, Sallie	Randolph.
109	Trawick, Hattie	Dale.
110	Trawick, James	Dale.
111	Underwood, William	Lauderdale.
112	Underwood, Lawrence	Lauderdale.
113	Vann, Martha	Madison.
114	Vickers, James	Henry.
115	Vines, Ada	Jefferson.
116	Wolf, Maggie	DeKalb.
117	Wolfe, Annie	Calhoun.
118	Wolfe, Helen	Calhoun.
119	Wolfe, Wash	Calhoun.
120	Williams, Atty	Marshall.
121	Williams, Lottie	Washington.
122	Yielding, Estelle	Jefferson.
123	Youree, William	Marengo.

N. B.—PRESENT NOVEMBER 10, 1892: Boys............46
Girls.............51

Total 97

ALABAMA ACADEMY FOR THE BLIND.

LIST OF PUPILS ENROLLED SINCE DATE OF LAST REPORT.

No.	Name.	County.
1	Alldredge, Enoch	Cullman.
2	Allen, Annice	Jackson.
3	Allison, Lizzie	Jackson.
4	Austin, Albert	Jefferson.
5	Baggett, Sallie	Monroe.
6	Baker, Lelia	Cherokee.
7	Bates, Winona	Bibb.
8	Beason, Joseph	St. Clair.
9	Cargile, Alice	Jackson.
10	Chamberlain, Fred	Jefferson.
11	Cocke, Wm	Chilton.
12	Darden, Elijah	Jefferson.
13	Davis, Dona	Henry.
14	Darlin, Joe	Shelby.
15	Darlin, Wm	Shelby.
16	Dill, Chris	Shelby.
17	DuVal. Emma	Marshall.
18	DuVal, Mary	Marshall.
19	England, Clifford	Choctaw.
20	Ennis, Tullic	Henry.
21	Farmer, John	Jackson.
22	Finney, John	Jackson.
23	Finney, Nannie	Jackson.
24	Finney, Monroe	Jackson.
25	Finney. Sarah	Jackson.
26	Frye, Maggie	Monroe.
27	Griffin, James	Jackson.
28	Hall, Eugene	Etowah.
29	Hall, Lily	Jackson.
30	Ham, Ambrose	Henry.
31	Haynes, James	Elmore.
32	Hicks, John	Henry.
33	Isbell, Sarah	
34	Jones, Gertrude	Jefferson.
35	King. Ida	Cherokee.
36	Knight, Clay	Jackson.
37	Kilgroe Mattie	St Clair.
38	Kreutzman, Bessie	Hale.
39	Lee, Daisy	Talladega.
40	Lee, James	Mobile.
41	Lorey, Willie	Jefferson.
42	Lovelace. Ben	Lauderdale.
43	Lucas, Tina	Barbour.
44	Malone, Ellen	Mobile.
45	Malone. Tom	Mobile.
46	McCollum, Gena	Clay.
47	McGehee, Jessie	Calhoun.
48	Moore, Earnest	Pike.
49	Moog, Isadore	Mobile.
50	Murphree. Kannie	Henry.
51	Orrell, Edwin	Mobile.

LIST OF PUPILS—BLIND—Continued.

No.	County.	County.
52	Parks, Lee	Jackson.
53	Pinson, Mildred	Jefferson.
54	Pinson, Eula	Coosa.
55	Pinson, Gregory	Coosa.
56	Pinson, Hixie	Coosa.
57	Pinson, James	Marshall.
58	Pinson, Rosetta	Marshall.
59	Pinson, Mollie	Marshall.
60	Pierce, Lily	Henry.
61	Pippin, Alice	Jackson.
62	Ray, Wm	Lauderdale.
63	Roebuck, Alfred	Shelby.
64	Roberts, Edward	Henry.
65	Runions, Robert	Calhoun.
66	Rush, Clarence	Lee.
67	Rush, Mollie	Lee.
68	Russell, Claude	DeKalb.
69	Self, Mary	Blount.
70	Scott, Jeff	Calhoun.
71	Sims, Minnie	Jefferson.
72	Sisk, Robert	Jackson.
73	Spivey, Robert	Mobile.
74	Swindell, Johnnie	DeKalb.
75	Tarrant, John	St. Clair.
76	Taylor, John	Montgomery.
77	Thomason, George	Jefferson.
78	Thompson, Lucian	Jefferson.
79	Williams, Tennie	Jackson.
80	Williams, Robbie	Jackson.
81	Williams, Thomas	Jefferson.
82	Williamson, Theo	St. Clair.
83	White, Laura	Lauderdale.
84	Whitely, Kate	Madison.
85	Winters, John	Jefferson.
86	Wishard, Myrtle	Madison.
87	Wycoff, John	Tallapoosa.
88	Yarbrough, Blanche	
89	Young, John	Lauderdale.

N. B.—Present Nov. 10, 1892.   Boys 29
                               Girls 27

              Total 56

ALABAMA SCHOOL FOR NEGRO DEAF-MUTES AND BLIND.

LIST OF PUPILS ENROLLED SINCE LAST REPORT.

DEAF-MUTES.

No.	NAME.	COUNTY.
1	Fain, Mary	Talladega.
2	Graham, Cap	Talladega.
3	Hill, Tillman	Talladega.
4	Jackson, Walter	Calhoun.
5	Jackson, Francis	Jefferson.
6	Matthews, Lula	Jefferson.
7	Matthews, Willie	Jefferson.
8	Morris, Willie	Calhoun.
9	Means, Augustus	Greene.
10	McLennon, Lewis	Calhoun.
11	Thomas, Woodson	Dallas.
12	Wade, Willie	Lauderdale.
13	Young, Joe	Jefferson.

Present November 10, 1892:   Boys.......... 9

Girls........... 4

Total............................ 13

BLIND.

No.	NAME.	COUNTY.
1	Allen, Tom	Jefferson.
2	Cheatham, Sherman	Escambia.
3	Fisher, Manassas	Jefferson.
4	Gardener, James	Jefferson.
5	Gardner, Henry	Dallas.
6	Glover, Ennis	Montgomery.
7	Grrett, Evans	Talladega.
8	Hilliard, Austin	Jefferson.
9	Jenkins, Katie	Talladega.
10	James, Jennie	Bibb.
11	Kellogg, Melton	Bibb.
12	Lacy, Lewis	Jefferson.
13	Madden, Ambrose	Lauderdale.
14	Pope, Mattie	Talladega.
15	Riddle, Tom	Greene.
16	Roebuck, Frank	Jefferson.
17	Stallworth, Eli	Conecuh.
18	Toney, Elijah	Montgomery.
19	Underwood, Isabella	Perry.
20	Winn, Henry	St. Clair.

Present November 10, 1892:   Boys.......... 13

Girls......... 7

Total............................ 20

TERMS OF ADMISSION.

1. No charge is made for pupils who are residents of the State of Alabama, except for clothing and traveling expenses.

2. Pupils are not admitted under eight years of age, and must be of good intellect and free from contagious or offensive diseases.

3. The session commences on the 15th of September, and closes on the 15th of June. The best time for admission is at the opening of the session. *Positively*, no pupil will be admitted after the end of the first quarter.

4. No pupil will be permitted to leave the Institution during the progress of the session without the consent of the Principal and Board of Commissioners.

5. Pupils are required to spend the vacation at home or with their friends. There is no exception to this rule. This arrangement is as desirable for the health of the pupils as for the convenience of the Institution.

6. The Institution is not responsible for pupils coming to or going from the Institution, or when they are truant from it. In such cases, however, all the assistance possible under the circumstances will be rendered.

7. *Entertainment* can not be furnished visitors or those accompanying pupils to the Institution. Good accommodation at reasonable rates can be had at the hotels and boarding houses in the city.

8. All communications should be addressed to the Principal of the Institute for the Deaf or the Superintendent of the Academy for the Blind.

J. H. JOHNSON,
Principal.

www.ingramcontent.com/pod-product-compliance
Lightning Source LLC
Chambersburg PA
CBHW021644270326
41931CB00008B/1159